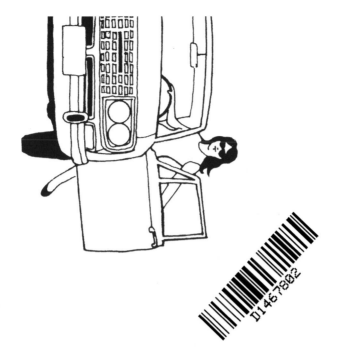

Willy Loman's
Reckless Daughter
or Living Truthfully Under Imaginary Circumstances

2015 Robert Dana-Anhinga Prize for Poetry

Selected by Maureen Seaton

to Ray Marscer with gratitude

Willy Loman's
Reckless Daughter

or Living Truthfully Under Imaginary Circumstances

Elizabeth A. I. Powell

*Johnson State College
14 September 17*

Anhinga Press
Tallahassee, Florida 2016

Cover art and design: Solidarity of Unbridled Labour
Author photo: Marion Ettlinger
Text design and production: Carol Lynne Knight
Type Styles: text set in Adobe Garamond Pro and titles set in Founders Grotesk

Library of Congress Cataloging-in-Publication Data
"Willy Loman's Reckless Daughter or Living Truthfully
Under Imaginary Circumstances" by Elizabeth A. I. Powell, First Edition
ISBN – 978-1-934695-49-4
Library of Congress Cataloging Card Number – 2016936301

Anhinga Press Inc. is dedicated wholly to the
publication and appreciation of fine poetry and other literary genres.

For personal orders, catalogs and information write to:
Anhinga Press
P.O. Box 3665
Tallahassee, Florida 32315
Website: www.anhingapress.org
Email: info@anhingapress.org

Published in the United States
by Anhinga Press
Tallahassee, Florida
First Edition, 2016

In memory of my parents,
Lindsey and Lewis Itkin

PRAISE FOR
WILLY LOMAN'S RECKLESS DAUGHTER
or Living Truthfully Under Imaginary Circumstances

Put Liz Powell's book on your must list. It's smart, bountiful word-luscious poems explore the fractious connections between daughters and parents, and men and women, and actors and audience, with a daredevil's brio and a philosopher's introspection; and the ambitious long poem that revisits/extends/unpacks *Death of a Salesman* is surely one of the finer pieces to come from Powell's generation of poets. It's a book to not just read, but to live in for a while.
— *Albert Goldbarth, author of "Selfish"*

These poems are pure METHOD, pure MADNESS: i.e. truth uncoupled from truth's invarience, self-evidence, and relativity. Powell is daughter, mother, and ex-wife, and the *f-ing* man: Miller and Miesner and Baron and Strasberg (and Strasberg) and Stanislavski and Diderot and Duse and Boleslawski and Adler and Rowlands and, yeah, a little Loman, too.
— *Olena Kalytiak Davis, author of "The Poem She Didn't Write and Other Poems"*

Whether constructing a metaphysical set design or deconstructing the human body into a question mark, Elizabeth Powell is an alchemist of letters. This book is a reminder of how many forms the poem can take — not only textually, but in the mind, the physical body and the spirit.
— *Melissa Broder, author of "So Sad Today"*

Elizabeth Powell brilliantly mines the psychodynamics of family life in *Willy Loman's Reckless Daughter*. These ambitious and deeply felt poems cohere through Powell's innovative adaptation of that mythic American narrative, *Death of a Salesman*. Powell's gift for strange and stunning turns of phrase and unexpected off-rhymes energizes the collection, and the recurring themes and motifs enhance its cumulative power.
— *Deborah Landau, author of "The Uses of the Body" and "Orchidelirium"*

CONTENTS

ACKNOWLEDGMENTS

My thanks to the publications in which these poems first appeared, sometimes in different versions:

Alaska Quarterly Review: "Will"

Bennington Review: "At the Swatch Watch Store, Newark Terminal C"

Blue Mesa Review: "Penultimate Condolence (originally as "First Letter from the Dead")

Green Mountains Review: "Willy Loman's Reckless Daughter"

Harvard Review: "Living Truthfully under Imaginary Circumstances: The Repetition Game"

Hobart (online): "Invitation to my Real Self from my Imaginary Self"

Hunger Mountain Review: "From the Joke Book of Condolences" (originally as "Fireside Chat")

Jet Fuel Review: "Regarding My Autopsy." "Condolence in Cement," and "Epilogue"

Mississippi Review: "The Curve"

The Missouri Review: "What Death Said," "Psychic Proem," "Traveling Salesman in Providence," and "Accident Report"

North American Review: "How to Sew an Unhemmed Day" (originally as "Lost Day")

Ploughshares: "On the Way to the Theater" (originally as "The Van")

Sugarhouse Review: "Funeral Staging"

"The Understudy's Soliloquies" appeared (in a different version) in *My Mother Married Your Father,* ed. Anne Burt, W. W. Norton, as "Infidelity."

Thanks to this book's many supporters, especially the incomparable Maureen Seaton, as well as the fabulous folks at Anhinga Press — Lynne Knight, Kristine Snodgrass, and Jay Snodgrass.

For their art and collaboration, thanks to Marion Ettlinger, Michael Jagger, Byron O'Neill, and W. David Powell. Indeed, many thanks to all my readers, colleagues, mentors, editors, students, friends, and family. Dr. Patricia Ferriera!!! Olena Kalytiak Davis!!! Deep gratitude to Tony Hoagland, Edward Hirsch, Albert Goldbarth, David Lehman, Melissa Broder, and Deborah Landau. Special hats off to Adrie Kusserow. I want to also thank Yaddo Corporation and Vermont Studio Center for time and support, as well as Johnson State College President Emerita, Barbara E. Murphy. Blessings to my siblings, Bird and Pickles, who have inhabited some of the same stages. And much love and special gratitude to my dear, dear children, always and foremost.

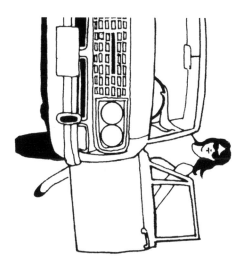

Willy Loman's Reckless Daughter

or Living Truthfully Under Imaginary Circumstances

The problem for the female-as-viewer, the female spectator, is how can she 'look' when the economy of the gaze is male? The problem may be briefly illustrated by providing an example from a theater context: Death of a Salesman.

— Elaine Aston

The Father. *We want to live.*

The Manager. *[ironically]. For Eternity?*

The Father. *No, sir, only for a moment ... in you.*

An Actor. *Just listen to him!*

Leading Lady. *They want to live, in us ...*

— Luigi Pirandello,
Six Characters in Search of an Author

ONE

Businessmen are serious.
— Allen Ginsberg

AUTOCORRECTING THE LYRIC I

I keep autocorrecting myself. I don't want to autocorrect myself. I autocorrect when I don't want to autocorrect. It disturbs the fusion of my interior monologue. I can't keep up with how fast things are changing. If I use autocorrect I am more suitable for you to see. I am dressed. I am not as naked as my fast typing might insist.

Autocorrection is a kind of conspiracy theory of reality based on the probability of words and un-nimble fingers. Thought is more easily rendered when you autocorrect, so it is said. But I know I am made from a God that makes homemade bread in the desert, even if He doesn't have yeast. I am not made of touchscreen typing, though it is didactic consideration. My fusion is a kind of Cupertino, inserted into the narrative even though it was never meant to be there. Yet, autocorrection is supposed reduce the probability I am wrong to you in the way Cary Grant never seems wrong to anyone.

When I autocorrect myself, it is better than back when I merely erased myself. There are many ways of erasure: deletion, drunk and disorderly, disintegration. Acting is a favored mode, and that's why I like theater, drama, monologue. I've had practice passing as a Jew *and* passing as a WASP because my math teacher explained that I am what used to be called in New York, a Mic-Moc, though I am not Irish. I have become kind of good at doing this passing, though the one identity is always trying to autocorrect the other. Can you guess which parent of mine is a Jew? A Gentile?

Let's say I'm fusion of cold borscht and finger sandwiches on white. I'm matzo ball Jew Bagel and thrifty Campbell's soup with dried parsley *don't-worry-about-me* luncheon. I'm noodle kugel and I'm turkey divan casserole. I'm Bubbeleh and I'm Dearie. I'm Ma and I'm Mummy. I'm the Episcojew, and I am strong and not strong! I have a family tartan and a silence in the Vilnius ghetto. I cannot be buried in the holy land, but I cannot be cremated. I am passing and have passed, heard the murmurs of *lovely* & also … *Dirty Jews, Fucking Gentiles*. I have paid close attention to speech and learned how to autocorrect instantly. As quickly as fire, which used to follow me around like a strange cat. Fire on the Amtrak from DC to NYC, fire in the living room burning the shag rug, *Fire on the Mountain* at the Dead Shows.

Now, I just keep turning my words into something else beside fire like someone with a personality disorder trying to make everything *look good!* It is humbling and uncool, but I keep trying to fill in the blank of myself with words that keep changing. It is better, the Boston Brahmins say, to have a history not a past, so when I speak in the "I" it must be my Jewish side, when I say that I am a vaudeville act in a quiet New England house. I'm the Daughter of the American Revolution in third class steerage. I'm the debutante in the Pogrom. I'm a morpher like autocorrection. I have tried to make myself acceptable to both sides. Literally.

I am an Elizabeth…I autocorrect into an *Electric*   *Elsewhere*

I am also Ann   *And   Another*

Powell to   *Power   Pose*

In Hebrew my name would be Bathsheba Bat Label

Bathsheba   becomes   *Banshee*   *Battery*

Also, I am delighted: Cary Grant was Jewish and Cary Grant was Church of England. He was perhaps the most successful autocorrector of all time. As a child he imagined himself (circumcision and all) as an English Gentleman, and so that is what he became.

I pass, and I self hate, and I take over the world with my great-grandfather's privilege and my great-grandmother's disappearance into the furnace of Eastern Europe with the *Protocols of the Elders of Zion*.

In the fall of 1970, the orange moth infested leaves made me scared of the sun. Under the "modern" swings with new plastic seats, the R.C. boys kicked me for "killing Christ," kicked me in my tartan kilt and patent leathers, right in the belly where my button should be. Dragged me down by my strawberry blonde to find the horns underneath.

I was stupid. I did not know my phone number yet. I was looking for my umbilical cord, but I had no umbilical cord.

When technology comes to help you it usually has a darkness underneath: (Think of Monopoly replacing gin rummy or Pampers causing all this asthma). No technology could help me autocorrect the fact I had absorbed my lost twin in utereo. He had died at some point. He died before anyone but me knew he even existed. Four months, maybe? And, it is said, the remaining fetus absorbs the bones and blood and memory of the other lost child. This happens all the time, like the way the word *Oligarchy* autocorrects into *Democracy*, and no one really thinks about it because they are typing their lives so fast they can hardly keep up with the minute hand. Another level of fusion. This is his fused monologue, too. I contain what might have been his speech, a kind of echolalia.

This is also why I always thought I had done something terribly, horribly wrong. So when the R.C. boys told me I killed Jesus Christ, I kind of believed them, not only metaphorically because we all have Pontius Pilot in us, but I also have my parents' first son inside my bones, and I miss him and know he contains an answer I need that has been autocorrected out of me to become a more pleasant word. Hence another autocorrection, though I keep writing "umbilical cord" and it keeps saying "umbilicus" or "umbrella" or sometimes "umpire," who always said "you're out!" So, then I decided I would write it out of the story, so I could become my doppelganger.

Somehow, though, the doppelganger must be female. When I speak of him and for him, it is a female voice because that is my gender. Wherever his Y went I do not know, only God does and that part is fine by me, although for a long time it scared me, like at any minute I might autocorrect into something else and not know why or how and be stuck. It was a matter of who was in control of the autocorrect any given day, ourselves, our God(s), the global consciousness of the sixties seeping up all around my childhood. I had a terrible fear that even if I never drank booze again, I would suddenly be struck drunk from magic autocorrection and black out and not know what I was doing. It was also a kind of OCD that survivors of dead twins in utero have. I read all about it on the Internet, so it must be true. I feared I might myself autocorrect the whole world like a Pac-Man figure bent on some propulsion much like an autocorrection that eats the world dot by pixelated dot.

Hence, I am suppressing myself and repressing myself. Ballet is the method I wanted most for this expression of control, but my Jewish grandmother danced with Martha Graham. I was not allowed to be a ballerina! Autocorrection. I am a modern dancer morphing/backflipping into (*ta-da*) GYMNAST! When I started bleeding at fourteen, I left it all for the large padded humiliation in my leotard and a bowl of hashish. I spent three hours with a box of Tampax. It was torture. These juxtapositions are creative memory, which is yet another way to say *autocorrection*.

Around then, I read my father's 1960s Compass copy of Arthur Miller's "Death of a Salesman" and began to understand why his sister called him Willy Loman. He had eaten the dream and it made him sick. I could hear my mother yelling, "No more 42nd Street hookers, no more secretaries!" The dishes would fly, and she'd be announcing "I am on my way to mother's!" That's when I noticed my doppelganger under the bed, snoring and talking and laughing in her sleep. "How could you laugh?" I said in the morning. "How could you not?" she said.

Some could argue it was a disjointed or multiple personality. It was around Passover and Easter when I, I mean we, were raped by the drunken neighbor Bill Gottlieb, who had tried to shoot his entire family because his wife modernized to using a potato peeler. I was so stupid, I still did not know my phone number.

It was more about intermarriage and the space between Passover and Easter when my doppelganger rose from the dead like Lady Lazarus and I didn't know if I should wear my cross or my Star of David. I didn't know like Cary Grant did that you could wear all the symbols on one gold chain if you wanted to.

My intermarried parents were divorcing; everything in society was splitting like a John Cheever story where the WASPS hung out drinking gin and tonics on the lawn. But my father's sister never stopped with the Willy Loman talk, and so we seemed to be acting that play as our family drama. I read it again and again, until the doppelgänger moved from under the bed to the top bunk.

It is said in writing "Death of a Salesman" that Arthur Miller was moved by his intermarriage and it made him think even more about assimilation. I'm sure he felt shame then about his Down syndrome child he kept secret.

But, it is always Biff Loman who has the most epiphanies on stage. Sometimes I think my brother, if he lived, might have been like Biff. Biff eats so much epiphany like birthday cake! He eats so much and leaves me only a sliver, he's eaten all the buttercream roses before I can even enter the stage on the elevator from my hell of guilt for killing Jesus Christ, by being the dregs of a legacy cured in Bourbon Old Fashioneds on an island off the coast of Maine not far from Blue Hill, and having relatives who chew chopped liver with mouths open. Biff can't hide who he is even if he uses failure to try and do it. The lost father makes a lost son, assimilated or not. I know all about it.

Like the rest of my immediate family, I am sure if Biff met me he would not like me. I imagine him as a kind of brother, though. For him, my voice has always been and will always be a kind of *shhhhhhhh*.

I've been stuttering this out a syllable a day — that's my wage as an abandoned child. Suddenly it seemed everyone exited stage left and right like the cartoon characters on the show I watched. I stayed home. I didn't want to ride over the Throgg's Neck to dreaded Long Island, where the dichotomies amplified to extreme. I was afraid of bridges until I realized I marched the Pettus Bridge in utero as my mother followed other marchers from behind in her knee socks and shorts and loafers, her secret gayness and dubious WASP empathy.

Eventually, I "grew up." For a long time I didn't understand my narrative so I yearned for a baby. When in doubt about the world, I liked to have babies and buy puppies.

My retinal flashes made no sense until I realized they were someone else's story trying to live through me. That sweet doppelgänger, brother-sister, evil other, good girl! The story kept banging at my red front door, the one I painted red for good luck, behind which I lollygagged and sofatized as I proceeded with the CNN-induced lobotomy dream of life. From CNN I learned autocorrect is a conspiracy theory because it keeps trying to change THE TRUTH! And I still didn't know my home phone number.

When I let my other HER SELF in the red door, she began dictating to me again, until we just used the auto-dictation on my MacBook Air —

> Sometimes I am an Elizabeth
> Sometimes she is a Bathsheba

I wanted to lie down in the back of my parents' 1970 Country Squire station wagon back when they put the seats down and the children slept without seat belts through the interstate night. But they have long since ridden down that highway, outta sight.

Cary Grant once said:

> *I made the mistake of thinking that each of my wives was my mother, that there would never be a replacement once she left.*

I understand this. This is what made me psychic. This is what makes images arrive on the doorstep with a bindle over the shoulder made of red bandana. Each man is the last man.

I search Wikipedia for an answer. Autocorrection is a kind of data validation, which "is the process of ensuring that a program operates on clean, correct and useful data. It uses routines, often called validation rules, validation constraints or check routines, that check for correctness, meaningfulness, and security of data that are input to the system."

Maybe my autocorrection has been a way for me to hide, to morph into whoever I was supposed to be in any given situation. The only thing I know is that Abraham is the only one who completely claims me in this story, I mean in addition to God.

The paradox of making a mockery of your self, to become not a mockery of your self. To devalue the capital of cool. To say: I am fucked up, is as old or older than Robert Lowell. I want you to "like" me because "J' suis Robert Lowell" or "J'suis Sylvia Plath." Let me say though that no one should autocorrect by killing herself. I love God this much (see my hands out as far as I can reach) and farther. Let this typing autocorrect me closer to him. He alone can turn a bad world into something useful. Let my autocorrect be the way you "batter my heart, Three Personed God." Please fill in my blanks in a way that pleaseth you my Lord, my one true only, God before any other Gods. I don't want to say, "Can I get an autocorrection!" I want to say, "Can I get an Amen?"

PSYCHIC PROEM-A-LOGUE

If you hold this poem up to the light, it can tell you
the latitude and longitude of where you stand.
If you place it under your pillow it interprets dreams:
It says a black horse means death, a white one, redemption.
It's concerned with processes outside physical and natural laws,
mostly theatrical. This poem once was my vanishing twin,
uses an oracle from *The Dream Book of Charms*
and Superstitions to speak to the dead. It likes to quote an old text
from the matriarchal Russian of our patriarchal side,
"Now a man, newly dead, would really know. And the poet
would bear witness to that knowledge, if only he could work out the way
of getting it." This poem identifies a long hall plastered with "don't
forget" Post-it Notes. It says this psychic reading may bleed ink,
that now it's forever an orphan, its mother was a lyric, its father a narrative.
It detects irregular heartbeats like cats detect earthquakes.
I know this poem is psychic because it told me I would write it when
I was typing letters in the secretarial pool on 290 Madison Avenue.
This poem detects an empty vehicle on the shoulder of I-95.
It wants to wedge itself between me and everyone else.
This poem paraphrases Nietzsche to test me: *He who fights*
with monsters should beware of becoming one.
This poem's jealous I attained flesh and it didn't.
This poem keeps trying to autocorrect the lyric "I."
This poem has a heart weighing 290 grams.
This poem contends money gone missing means
three things: sex, booze, gambling. It claims
it once helped Willy Loman make a sale. This poem preaches
only love is redemptive. This poem is made of me and I it. It doesn't worry
about irony or stance, only odd incidence and fact, and doesn't care
if it tells the truth about what will happen to my face
or behind my back. It says all time happens simultaneously.
This poem feels my heart grow heavy in its chest, wondering if it makes

good decisions, loves the right ones rightly, leaves the wrong ones deftly.

This poem says: *I'm a door, but don't turn the knob clockwise.*

This poem hears me think, and knows my strictest secret. It says:

Dial 1-800-F-O-R-T-U-N-E for only 99 cents per minute.

It is psychic because it predicts the next clue in the next poem.

This poem meets my eyes and says: try me.

CARE PACKAGE, WITH RIDDLE AS MISSIVE

I found my father's favorite Swiss army knife
in a box he sent me with no note,
just James Bond videos,
nothing else.
What was the message?

The message was there wasn't one.

This world violent, full of sex,
the movie's zeitgeist, era after era, a new Bond
double-o-seven-ing in.

Divorced dad Sundays
at The Greenwich watching
the British Secret Service save the world.

I thought he sent the knife inadvertently,
but now I see it was code —

he was boxed in
without a knife
to cut himself out.

LIVING TRUTHFULLY UNDER
IMAGINARY CIRCUMSTANCES

The goal of the Meisner acting technique has often been described as getting actors to "live truthfully under imaginary circumstances." Here are some acting games we have found useful.

I.
THE REPETITION GAME:
The Moment is a Tricky Fucker

In the repetition game you repeat what I say. Sometimes you change it and then make me repeat it until we are joined in *moment*.

Hello: Hello.
Goodbye: Goodbye.

In this warehouse loft, windows are as tall as walls. Outside, the trees repeat each other's call to the sky. Their roots bank their secret messages in the earth. I am your spontaneous responder, and you are my spontaneous responder. We go on like this until one of us needs a sip of water.

We came here through the old neighborhood, took three lefts. There is a crack in your lower lip that bleeds out a truth you won't repeat back to me. Our poetic problem is to enact a relational philosophy of each other. This is how beings can be made.

We both want to be whole, so the story can be told. We are engaging in a kind of process theology with each other, like others engage in sex or eating or drinking.

This is where our intention is to make this a prologue exercise that defines the trajectory of our story, as if we have always been together not merely as characters.

I am Willy Loman's Reckless Daughter.   (I repeat).

I'm a doppelgänger, step-sister, bitch, bastard — the roofied one, erased from the storyline.   (You repeat).

I've got stage fright, which is a kind of trauma of having to be born again. (I repeat).

I hear footsteps on the fire escape, but it is only our voices reverbing against the mirror behind the ballet bar. A speckled green vase on the farmhouse table painted black yelps for admiration by the door.

THEOTHERWOMAN/ Our Mother always asking (off-stage): "Are you paying attention to what I am saying?"

You say: "Are you paying attention to what I am saying?"

So, I say it. My double, my sister: We are engaging in an energy event. I am disassociating into you. God is an actor acting on us: You are inventing me and I am inventing you. Where have you been? I say. Where have you been? You say.

"Your hair's a mess: Brush it."
"Brush it!" (THEOTHERWOMAN/Our Mother says off stage).

A little brown starling on the sill. A zigzag of scratches on this old pine floor.

Our poetic problem is to enact a relational philosophy of each other. This is how beings can be made.

Sails can be heard clinking against masts in the harbor behind us.

We both want to be whole, so the story can be told. We are engaging in a kind of process theology with each other like others engage in sex or eating or drinking.

"Here's the brush."
"Do you want the brush?"
We have no trigger words. All words are trigger words, that's how we like it. Real.
"Don't brush your hair by the food. I'll give you the brush, then you'll cry."

A fruit basket encased with plastic wrap by the industrial sink: green apples, navel oranges, an unripe pineapple doesn't solve our hunger. The mirror is our dining table, pull up that black metal chair.

Are you paying attention to what I am saying? I'll give you the brush.

This is where our intention is to make this a prologue exercise that defines the trajectory of our story together, as if we have always been together not merely as characters. We know where the typewriter is. (It is hidden in the closet.)

Is there something you want to tell me?

This is where we might read our Alfred Whitehead philosophy grandfather gave us and say: "Your creating makes no difference to God's existence, only to God's of me." But after you repeat me, you say:

I want to have a Godsperience —

So, I'm writing a ritual to bring back our father in some form because God is an actor in our story.

The OTHERWOMAN/ Our Mother (still off-stage) says: Are you listening to what I am saying?

You call to me, and I repeat what you say.

I've got stage fright, which is a kind of trauma of having to be born again.

You bite a green apple vigorously. I open the window to prove myself to the wind. *We are listening.* It is autumn again. Five minutes ago it was spring.

You don't impersonate a character, you personate a character.

I want to be whole again, so I begin *living truthfully under these imaginary circumstances* with her.

I am the stranger in the mirror in conversation with my doppelganger.

We proceed to the next exercise.

II.
THE ANIMAL EXPERIMENT: Ways to Be

You are an ELEPHANT in this experiment. You are the man who plays Willy Loman heavy with a gray burden.

You are inhabiting an ELEPHANT, so that you can inhabit the play. The elephant wears a gray suit and seems so sad.

ELEPHANTS die of loneliness every day. When I am lonely, I too, pretend I am an ELEPHANT.

I am THE GIRL CHILD in the play, but have been written out of the play. I am supposed to pretend to be a MOUSE.

MOUSE, slang for girl or woman or black eye. Girl so small you can hardly see her. Hidden, secret, she squeaks in darkness.

If you want to express it another way, a MOUSE can be a nautical thing closing off the load so it doesn't slip off the hook.

Mice die of being a dime a dozen every day.

When I am a dime a dozen, I too, pretend I am a MOUSE. MOUSE (small details in a big picture) and ELEPHANT (big picture in small details), but that is an old story about perception.

Why should a MOUSE scare an ELEPHANT so?

Is it because the ELEPHANT like the computer can be controlled by an object that has fine control of a graphical user interface?

MOUSE (high frequency) or ELEPHANT (low note/frequency).

Ganesh is the ELEPHANT God, the remover of obstacles. When you want to be magnificent you pretend you are Ganesh. This gets you a standing ovation.

The mice like a multitude of sudden autumn hail.

But the one thing both City Mice and Country Mice know is this: *Better beans and bacon in peace than cakes and ale in fear.*

In Rumi's poem about an ELEPHANT and a blind man one thing is clear:

One's subjective experience can be true, but that such experience is inherently limited by its failure to account for other truths or a totality of truth.

This is at the crux of the drama, especially of a character in search of an author who tried to erase her after he invented her.

Once you have acted on a stage you aspire to other stages, too.

It is only on stage the self you have known whispers from back in the canyon of your childhood. She understands why we must play in order to understand God.

Play is the child's work. The child is God. Play is the enactment of the liturgy.

Offstage everything else is parable.

The father may or may not welcome us home, slaughtering the fatted calf and offering the family signet ring.

The lighting is suggesting we might also like poetry, Whitman, maybe even each other.

On stage, a multitude has one loud-large voice: that is why we believe the MOUSE can be as mighty as the ELEPHANT.

Both die equally of loneliness.

In the beginning, there was an *introduction*, which is close to *induction,* into this splintered personality, splintered the way light contains all colors.

At various times, the parable has provided insight into the relativism, opaqueness or inexpressible nature of truth, but what about the MOUSE who tries to climb the summit of the ELEPHANT?

Whatever the MOUSE sees is his perception of truth from such a small angle. But, what insistence! And that's the desire to know oneself from the outside-in.

In short, we like fables because we like a useful truth. We like the large power of sadness, the small power of a dime-a-dozen. The magic *if* turning to the magic *is*.

III.
OBJECTS OF ATTENTION: The Key to Real Emotions

Unless we open the book, we can't have real emotions.

In the book, there are *Objects of Attention*.

THE OTHERWOMAN. Silk stockings (also known as shears), ghosts, a valise, New England road maps, a receptionist's desk.

"Are you paying attention to what I am saying?"

THE OTHERWOMAN provides access to the scene. But the access is exploitation. SEX. Here THE WOMAN is our mother.

THE OTHERWOMAN says you ruined her, so she will give you directly to the buyers.

Access is buying into the buying.

My mother said, "Are you paying attention to what I am saying?"

Paying attention means to purchase mindfulness of the moment at a cost.

What is the cost?

The cost is our witness.

Look, look in the valise. It is an object of attention.

What is it they are buying?

Aspects of the splintered mind? Our broken father?

We know each other, you and me.

We are still in the warehouse loft. The windows have darkened with shadow's medicine. The mirror has befriended us.

Maybe you should open the VALISE!

On stage looking for an object of attention.

Pay attention! The object might be the KNOCK ON THE DOOR.

Flashback: Silk stocking (also known as sheers), garden variety seeds, a football, a steak dinner, a car crash.

An expressionistic nightmare as an object of attention.

The object of attention is in the *valise-valise-valise*.

Or maybe the object of attention is: "*Maybe the hotel is on fire?*"

Witness to his failure, Miss Francis was THE WOMAN.

THE WOMAN is my mother, her mother. A buyer. She buys what Willy is selling. This is the kind of stock we spring from. We are the imposition of the will through selling.

"The woods are burning" is what he is selling, mostly to us.

For that particular minute, the object of our attention is a burning forest. But we hear laughing. The response is always laughing. Laughter becomes an object for us to attend to. In the moment. The now is a laugh.

THEOTHERWOMAN is always laughing in the bathroom or Willy is shoving her into the hallway naked.

THEOTHERWOMAN in Boston. She is our mother. She is: Not a "chippy." Not a "strudel." She is not your girl. She is not "on-call."

The deal is I (we) have failed math like THE SON has failed math, and he (our father) has failed marital fidelity because his addition is all wrong. He is a subtraction problem his offspring are trying to solve.

So he becomes the object of our attention in most everything. We know each other, you and me, sister. It takes a lifetime to untangle these wires. Even the great playwright knows creation is about sex.

Our mother, THEOTHERWOMAN, lived with her sisters. Our mother was a witness to his failures. Her payment for his sex was silk stockings.

The object: Why do rapists maim with stockings?

THEOTHERWOMAN is our mother and is a secret herself.

THEOTHERWOMAN is hidden to audience and to wife, but not to us, to me, her illegitimate daughter.

She "took that phony dream and burned it before something happened."

The Father desertion leaves you "feeling temporary about yourself."

The Dream is male in this construct.

The object of our attention is the dime on the floor, stuck in a syrupy black stain.

"I'm not a dime a dozen!" our father yells. But THEOTHERWOMAN knows, "God creates the world by informing it with possibilities" & that "it lies in the nature of all things that many may enter into complex unity."

The object of our attention is this dream that turns out to be real. The object of our attention is at once the object of our attention and also ourselves.

THEOTHERWOMAN: "Are you paying attention to what I am saying?"

The Object of Attention is this BOOK that I am writing and have written. It is 6 x 9 with numbered pages. If they'd open the valise (no matter the year), they'd find it under the sheers, the lingerie, the road maps, the laughing and the burning.

The object of our attention is Yeatsian: "How can we tell the dancer from the dance?"

A horrible thing to have your mother's script.

IV.
SENSE MEMORY: (Re)-Experiencing Time Travel

NOT ACT but ACTUAL. I am trying to WILL an EMOTION by inhabiting objects like space and time and a hallway.

Back to basics. What color is it? The smell of that day?

Scenework: Crystals forming around the window, old mold begins to freeze. The taste of Mallomars on the tongue.

Yesterday was a yellow room day, a holiday of candles and butter. The good thing that always happens before the bad in magical thinking.

The taste of butter turning rancid. The lilies dying in the vase, smelling like compost and rain. The scent memory of my innocence turning toward experience.

Scenework. I see this and smell this experience from life so that I may make the past live again.

When I say I am the UNDERSTUDY I am not taking responsibility for my life.

Scenework: I remember wearing purple Danskin slacks with an elastic waist. I was holding a book. I had taken a sip of each discarded drink from the "grown-up party" & was playing "tea-time." Juniper berries and plastic.

Scenework: Creating a parallel event/persona. I have a strong want to be "unburdened." Sometimes "she" goes to some other part of "myself."

I'm serious about this. I'm not sure why she now has become so obsessed with me, this other one that I want and don't want.

I have read enough books on recovering from being well-oiled that I know I must stop being the understudy, but this is incredibly difficult.

I have more personalities than a ROLODEX has business cards. I was blotto because I was shattered in the way the Rolling Stones sing about it. In the way a small child is who is taken into a room with an ex-convict and made to drink peppermint schnapps and lie on his polyester orange and yellow bed and black out until she walks from the room and is shown his medals of valor from a war she doesn't understand. She didn't know peppermint that way until she came to dislike the sunniest days.

This is called disassociating. It is a kind of playacting that turns what is unacceptable into something that might be interesting.

I'm serious about this. Sometimes "she" goes to some other part of "myself."

Disassociating makes it possible for me to travel the space-time continuum and inhabit other actors and have them inhabit me even though my central personality stays intact.

I ask her, THE DOPPLEGÄNGER: Were you ever in a polyester room in a brick tenement on top of a hill with a window that looked out into a playground of happy children?

Our MOTHER: Are you paying attention to what I just said?

Yes, I think you might be implying that disassociating is a kind of dreaming meditation.

Our MOTHER has said in-between her lines that method is a means of grace, a way to disappear into public ritual.

I ask her, THE DOPPLEGÄNGER: Were you ever in that room that smells of Aqua Velva and old man and polyester curtains and dust? Were you ever in the room of shag rug and distilled vapor of gin? The room of paint pigment smelling of old news? The room across the hall from the wall that divided the apartments between light and dark?

I know you were there. Are you paying attention to what I just said? I begin to steal my mother's lines.

Scenework: Trauma (related to Drama).

Scenework: That was the day you began to be created. You were not another personality like in the movie that scared me, "Sybil." No, you really were separate from me, but we've lived this life somehow since that room. You are not bad, but you set out to push us to every precipice you could find.

Yes, this is part of your recklessness. You like to take opportunities inside of creation and scold them, so that God thinks we are ungrateful.

The crux of evil in process theology says there are moments of possibility for good that we haven't taken advantage of. Something like that.

In method acting: "They were given a single line of dialogue, told to turn away, and instructed not to do or say anything until something happened to make them say the words (one of the fundamental principles of the Meisner technique).”

Yet, the goodness was there all the time, but someone put their darkness around the field like an eclipse.

So I/you dared each blessed gift from creation to show you that it really loved you by making choices toward the way you didn’t really want to go. You let the darkness push the automatic button. Bad idea. So here we are, characters again searching for our author, so we can act in the play that might have been. A possibility of choices and free will. That’s what acting is.

“Are you paying attention to what I am saying?” the DOPPLEGÄNGER takes up saying now, too.

I’ve got stage fright, which is a kind of trauma of having to be born again: *ma semblable, ma soeur.* It’s not over if the problem isn’t solved. All stories are secrets.

Where is your ELEPHANT God now my little MOUSE? Didn’t (y)our half-brother Biff say:

I saw the things that I love in this world. The work and the food and the time to sit and smoke. And I looked at the pen and I thought, what the hell am I grabbing this for? Why am I trying to become what I don’t want to be … when all I want is out there, waiting for me the minute I say I know who I am.

It is then the house lights dim for the drama to begin again — extinguish our lives for another two out-of-body hours in the sea of orchestra section, thrown over the life boat into script, into the spotlight spectacle, in the dark, waiting for truth, instead of what is felt.

We hold our lives like a playbill. Wondering if our father can imagine acting every truth denied, knowing every verity from a new vantage point.

We (I) walk stage after stage, each act a compass aiming true north. To live truthfully under imaginary circumstances is to understand what Einstein said: *All time is simultaneous.*

How the pebble dropping to the ocean floor, one with every grain of sand, discovers its parental continental slope, that the truth *is*.

ACCIDENT REPORT

Low man on the road, the crow caws sung you out.
Traveling Northbound on I-95, center lane.

The frenzied dogs' discordant barking null and voided you.
Vehicle veered left due to operator impairment.

A single, skeletal roadside phlox swaying in truck-wind waved you out.
Operator grazed the guard rail, stopped vehicle on left shoulder.

Your angora socks, your Aquascutum decked you out.
Operator mental and physical status: Unconscious.

The Kool menthols smoked you out.
Apparent contributing factor: operator illness.

The Exit 4 diner's smell of Sunday morning bacon fixed your fate.
Full daylight visibility, road conditions: clear.

The bare trees, the impending snowstorm sold you out.
Identified operator upon arrival.

The lonely towns you passed, their closed offices, crossed you out.
Male, Age 61, Driver's License number T5143988.

Your unanswered pager's insistent beeping crossed you out.
EMTs try resuscitating heart attack victim at site.

The gawking onlookers crossed you out.
Operator vital signs flatline.

Every present tense verb crossed you out.
Car at State Police barracks impounded, pending reclamation.

SET DESIGN: WHAT THE DOOR KNOWS

The door is clairvoyant. It doesn't need the fingerprints
to know. The door knows whom the unknown will shroud next,
its rust creaking hinge pontificating. No one understands
just how much this door knows. Its lintel provides a hint:
Weary is the man who knows his fate.

The door's every rumbling atom fueling
each seismic prophecy. If you breach
this doorway, beware of treading on its sill;
carefully turn its burning handle clockwise.
This door made of nails and glue, smooth white paint,

a lock that always sticks. This door discerns the dates
of all who pass. It knows the manner and details
of your death. It screeches its witness. You will know it
by the lead paint chips flaking from its frame,
and it will grant your coming or going before you do.

TRAVELING SALESMAN IN PROVIDENCE

His character weighed on a balancing scale, suspended between null and void.

He couldn't desert his wife despite her spite. His mistress, half his age,

required Viagric stamina. He didn't want to strap her

to an old man, who'd soon grow bald and foolish. The facts swelled

his aorta, sped his blood toward its restless dying. The autumn air

smelled of allegory, a foreshadowing before curtains draw shut.

CNN blued his room with its bituminous glow. He grappled

the aging man's cliché, wrestled at forty, a mood —

What was the world coming to? His High Mass of Selling

became a weary road. Dazed by the tube, the same old Chinese food,

he hungered to elect a new life, but the spicy stir-fry of *what-might-be*

gave him heartburn. His arches killing him, perspiration quenched the dread.

At first, he assumed — panic attack — uncertainty's impending doom,

narrowing the stage and scene, his hotel room.

The Haitian cleaning lady helped him to the lobby from his bed

to await the ambulance; it wasn't heartburn or in his head.

His inaccuracies left him dangling; his secrets, sweet and accidental,

cost him all he claimed. He no longer believed in the God of optimism.

A small man can be just as exhausted as a great man. He'd sell the same

wholesale wreck, the same story in Boston for now. He watched

the meltdown of his inner-core from the theater of his brain.

PERFORMANCE REVIEW

Just a conversation over an Americano.

Networking, she said, as if the word were an angel hovering.

A thought bubble of seduction capital was rising:

He was market researching his soul's out of body experiences.

Another come-to-Jesus meeting in due time.

Competition always asked the same questions:

But could he get it done by Friday?

Done & done!

Could he use some brand storytelling with his thunderbolt thinking?

Yes. Yes — absolutely.

He was living with decisions that required him to be "that guy."

Did he know how to fly a Cessna like Brad Pitt?

Yes — of course. A win-win:

It was early spring in the garden of low hanging fruit.

Gender parachutes were storyscaping the wide avenue outside.

He didn't want to be blamed for being cruel, only a bit cerebral.

She said which one are you:

Visionary motivator? Clarifier of perception? External brander?

No one wants to be vanilla and without crosspollination,

he professed. Deliverables were what was important,

that and a few good corporate sponsors.

Sounds like, she said, you have lots of ways to be engaged.

His handshake said it had been one of the worst winters.

She wanted a freshness update on his newsjacking efforts,

next time, when Pumpkinspicelattes would come back on line.

She left him for a photo shoot uptown at the Guggenheim.

ON THE WAY TO THE THEATER, STUCK IN A ROUNDABOUT

Where the fuck are we? Father asks. We've been translated into a language we didn't quite understand. There's a tractor on the side of the road, with a seat for an especially large ass. It rains. Father says the rain holds certain nuances the language never can. We try to deliver a message to the German relatives of my father's new wife.

At the traffic circle that loops around a monument of a soldier on horseback. Father drives round & round the circle whistling, eating Swiss chocolate — *around and around oblivion we go. ...* I count silently in my head, one hundred and ten, then say: *Do you realize how many times we've gone around this thing?* Father says, *Nevermind*, there's a handbag bazaar just ahead, *I know it's here somewhere.* We pass the same gas station twice. *You drive like Jerry Lewis.* He hands me a map, but nothing matches. We want to know where the fuck the miracle is.

Sanctified by our weird love of the roundabout, we go around and around. We bob like corks in water, our Euro Van filled with light matter on the way to Brecht. Our lack of suspension wants to cure us of every emotional malady with its focus on the physical as we jostle together around and around.

We surrender to the thrashing, thrust all at once into the left side. I dream of beds, different lives, lunch. We are imaginary people becoming real once again by the fever of this throttle: Some Jewish men just *love-love-love* blonde shiksas.

We have traveled here out of a confused duty that neither Freud nor Jung could have untangled. Father says it is a love of History. Travel has settled nothing, neither has assimilation. Neither has Father. We have returned to this freaky old farmhouse Europe sticky with stale beer, and it feels like an acid trip gone postmodern-bonkers.

Father is a good Reform Jew. We are going to the theater instead of the synagogue. No shock absorbers with this van; we're resigned to that now. Vertiginous, but determined, we can imagine no other way; another scene will come of this, somehow. It does.

I try not to hate my beautiful Germanic stepmother who keeps putting lip-gloss on in the visor mirror. I try not to let my eyes meet hers there. I can't help but see what's missing in the skyline, the darkening question of how each of us will survive this feeling of air that jostles us further apart until we are sick to our stomachs, dizzy with what is, what was and what is to come.

I see an old woman dressed in black, laughing. I hear the screeching of a metal swing. Finally, I see a sign. I translate: *Tourist Leather!* We park the car and Father buys handbags for his new German relatives. We ask the salesman for directions upon which we are translated and transported *into a different part of the story* when he speaks Russian and points left.

It is snowing to the left, and all the hotels are full, except for one that looks like a castle. In its restaurant, the white-aproned maître d' seats us next to a table of two young Germans, cousins of my new stepmother, who ask me about Las Vegas. I have never been to Las Vegas. My father buys drinks and gives the handbags to their mother, wife of a retired SS officer, who helped round-up Jews, my real cousins.

Later, after the play, though it's late, Father won't go to bed, but stays up drinking, the wine translating what this encounter means to us, now he's married into it. Still his own mother won't ride in his Volkswagen. I think of Brecht, of Celan. Is it moral to write of beauty in a time of tragedy? Father's new relatives use some words his lousy German couldn't parse — his head spinning like an outdated globe asking, *Where am I?* He had no idea, although before he passed out he said the daisies on the bar looked frighteningly familiar.

FUNERAL STAGING

Scene 2.

Your grave was one of your hotel rooms paid for by credit cards:
Click and swipe, the plastic feeling of not-all-right. What you called
my Madame Alexander doll face, expressionless. New Hampshire
Land Rovers circled like ravens, your tribe arriving to see you lowered
into the hole in my chest. While my newborn suckled me, I sat
on the metal mourner's chair. A sky-deep silence pushed you so far,
you fell in. My ears would not pop. Instead of roses, I threw in thirteen cities.
The Holiday Inn, parts of I-95 North. Providence, Boston, Northampton,
Brattleboro, my compunction and the State of Maine. Concord, then
Waterbury. I threw in lies, truths, rants, hangovers, my good girl attempts,
a Pan Am 747, your horn-rimmed glasses, passport. Your boar bristle
hairbrush, blood pressure pills, travel alarm clock, your genetic loneliness,
your *Tinker-Tailor-Soldier-Spy,* Chinese take-out menus,
Michelin guides, Marx Brothers screen saver, PalmPilot,
 mustache trimmer, shoe horns, suit press, road weariness.

Scene 1.

Frost heaves form under the subconscious of the road home, not far
from this cemetery, where once on the cold, cold shoulder you stopped
the car and soliloquy'd at me to *get the fuck out*. Mother had slammed
the door on the Western world for good in her rendition of Ibsen;
I acted out the biblical, the prodigal doll returning to our cold dollhouse.
Always returning: Another long trip into one of our arguments
following us like suspicious cops. The road's thumping metronome
sounds like your aggravated heartbeat, and something overheating
that smells as acrid as ire. Sometimes premonition is just staging:
I try to jump from the moving car as you downshift, then up ahead see
an overturned Audi. The driver pleading through our reflections
while you try to break the glass, shout *Get back*, but it is useless,
everything is about to blow. We don't speak of it, but each silently
imagines the death of the other. How to live? That was the question.

THE CURVE

The Daughter drove it slowly, downshifting, watching for wet leaves, blinding storm of visible/invisible. No matter is ever destroyed. His hand on her shoulder (invisible or not) said she could pass any obstruction safely.

The curve was like a scythe. The curve was something that blindsided but was elegant, extreme. The curve was a man quickly waving her on, quickly waving hello, quickly waving goodbye.

Many believe the curve can read the future, that to inherit the curve means total knowledge. The curve is the working mind, but is also not the working mind. The curve has something to do with second and minute hands. She drove into the bend of it, slowly, like he said, downshifting.

He was teaching the Daughter how to drive. His briefcase at his feet. He said never mind people with Ivy League educations, they can't sell a thing. He said never hide your drink. He said in the end there's always Mexico, and also never sleep your way to the top. Watch where you're going. And then,

the Daughter sped up to follow the grace note of slope, extending in what seemed like the infinite. But it wasn't her infinite, not yet. The curve was still an arc and she was a compass drawing the curve with her pointed toes, hand on the ballet bar, second position, she downshifted, like he said. She thought she would never stop this dancing. She was racing you to the top. The gears were grinding.

For the curve also became her body stretching itself out from childhood, where she stood amazed, hips-waist-breasts-hair, in front of the long fairy tale mirror, curious about the trip she was embarking upon. The way she pulled out of the curve then and into the sing-song vroom of the downshifting into the next curve, again, like he said.

Don't ride the clutch, be sure. He said, watch out for wet leaves in spring.
His hair turned, suddenly, whiter. He said, don't completely trust the
mirrors. He said turn around to see who is behind you.

The curve was a slap in the face. The curve was the moon casting spells.
The curve was an orange rind. The curve was half a valentine. The curve
was a message coded and unclear. The curve was anticipation. The curve
was a curtain on the stage. The curve was who she would become

after Act One. The curve within it contained a crash. The curve was
the inside of his Brooks Brother's suit coat, the silk of it. The curve was
his Achilles' heel. The curve was the Blood calling out from the ground,
biblical and true. The curve was a hand cupping itself under running water.

She drove into the bend, slowly, like he said, downshifting. The curve
was the tracing of the back of her neck. The curve was the passing over.
The curve was the approach into the forest. The curve was the hunter
stepping out into virgin snow. The curve was the bow string pulled back

and ready to release. The curve was the surface of the earth as it turned
toward the sun. The curve was the rushing of the spring over the fields.

The Daughter drove into the bend slowly. The sound of a train's whistle,
a tire screech. The curve was the cervix, now dilating to ten. The curve
was the head beginning to descend.

But the curve was not a birth. The curve was not a death. The curve
was not the animal brought out of the woods. The curve was not the
empyrean or the stars shaped into a premonition. The curve was a
question mark. The curve was a crash. The curve was when he said;
speed up when coming out of the curve.

He said this, so that death, close behind, would be left in the curve as the road began to narrow. He said, here are the keys, it's yours now. The Daughter drove into the bend slowly, like he said, downshifting, ahead and up into the glorious hills.

PSYCHOANALYSIS OF FIRE: TORCHING THE FOURTH WALL

> — *noun: the space that separates performer*
> *or performance from audience.*

The Doctor is breaking down the fourth wall again: The wall that's invisible and says you mustn't speak directly to the audience. The audience — many angels threading the long tale together. Theater, like fire, can fuse anything. The tug of war with what you are and what you pretend to be.

The curtain wants to shut itself because it is ablaze in its psychoanalytic red velvet. The man who plays the Doctor is reassuring in his tweed-n-pipe. He says: Don't assume all your thoughts are true. Sometimes fire lies as it flames the friction between two things. He says: all theater is violence to the real.

The Doctor believes *Playbills* are elegant procedure because people like to believe the future is in their hands, but the Doctor knows the future is on fire, too, and that this is called *reverie.* The Doctor is always asking the Daughter: *Tell me about your father.*

The Daughter takes out her eyes and hands them to the Doctor. Fire is intuition. The Doctor sets his eyes in the clean ash tray and puts her eyes in. It is effortless. It is well-acted. Their middle-class sincerity hovers like the USS Enterprise.

The Doctor and the Daughter have tried the *Empty Chair Technique,* now the *Mirror Technique,* where the double gives concrete suggestions such as where on stage to stand. The Daughter believes in silk stockings, in playing tricks, in dancing the tarantella, but the Doctor does not. The Doctor believes in the invisible line of trauma, in the ability to cross that line.

The Doctor suspects some go to the stage like some go to the altar. The Doctor asks: *sleeping? eating? hearing voices?* The Daughter detects she's been written out of another classic American situation. The Doctor wants to know how this makes her feel, fumbles to retrieve his own eyes back, because he does not know what he is seeing. He has no idea how dangerous narrative can become to perception.

EPILOGUE

This reckless daughter
       kept using *I* statements.
You were turning off

the auditorium lights were headlights
shattering   sound of the switch
brake ignition ditch

       The stage was an abandoned car wreck
The scene stuttering   what happened?

Sirens wailed the cops' arrival — I was using *I*
statements to call 911,   but they merely inquired
about stage direction, location,
character motivation.

They advised all ghosts
exit the ramp   or the trick door stage right

but the ghosts were under union
contract stagehands delivering scripts
to the unconscious   the way
drama always works —

you're unaware of something
you know, but walk toward it

because secrets are symmetrical,
yellowheadlights   wintershatter
       hysterical daffodils waving
early spring   ActOneTwoThree
come and gone like lust, there must be

a debriefing where you try
          talking me down from the stage
as if you talked another kind of actress from a ledge,

          the feeling of falling out   that window

until   the waking
older men, legs in aisle   round heads   moons
light sleep
          someone should Supreme Court scream   *Fire*
in this theater they never do.

I had to live the truth   even if it ruined the play
          Still   that one   non-metaphoric light
on you.   Spotlight   searchlight
          coplight   foresight
          it is truth

or some version of avoiding it,
          compelled like a sex-addict-badass-poet-pothead
bad childhood   car-wrecked dead businessman.
          I kept using *I* statements

you doing what didn't work
over and over
as if

welding a car from the staged smashup
headlights   sirens   moons   balconies.
I dropped to my knees, but no audience

heard — only the sleeping men and
　　　　my soliloquy of me
passing like roadside trees
　　　　Cherryblossomsnow
bridge down　　　　　　road out　　　　　　　　oil slick

For our acting technique　　　　　we fooled ourselves,

asking the same things
　　　　those ghosts had,
ghosts that looked　　　　　　　like us.

Under the grave of the symphony pit,
invisible　　　　music to which we danced,

made-up,　　　　costumed,　　　I entered the secret
with a key, banged on it with authority —
　　　　as if we weren't invisible

a dialogue tag　　　　　　for a dog tag
you　　　tried to put on the directional signals the emergency
　　　　　　　　light　　　on/off/on/off

You said: Come on say it already,
before you hemorrhage at the scene.

TWO

Every entity is to be understood in terms of the way it is interwoven with the rest of the universe.
— Alfred North Whitehead

We do on stage things that are supposed to happen off, which is a kind of integrity, if you look on every exit as being an entrance somewhere else.
— Tom Stoppard

THE UNDERSTUDY'S SOLILOQUIES

In the first pew, a fistfight brewed, bitter like cheap coffee,

scorched on a warming plate. A nephew proclaimed Khadafy-like:

this is fucking boring! The crucifix draped in black, improvisational,

per the traveling Rabbi's requirements for performing in a Congregational

church the mitzvah making funeral. Stepmother's veterinarian nephew,

mocked me at the lectern. My Tony Soprano brother said: *oh, bless you* —

NOT! and almost allotted him his teamster style uppercut punch.

The photo on top of Father's coffin was from before the creditcrunch,

a portrait taken for a *New York Times* article on American business.

Father fake-smiled from the frame before his final stage left. His mistress

in the back made eye contact with the idea concealed behind journalistic

facts. We were those *who-what-where-when-hows,* mystic and synergistic,

carried by birth into this improvisation, theatrics of interstices,

cosmic stratagems of sales sheets, minute particulars, invoices.

I didn't mean to be his understudy following along to the transliteration
of Hebrew, poetry meant to sing him to a different realm of imagination.
We were tucking him in now, the Rabbi said. *That's what orphans
do.* Alive he might have said: *Give me my stage or give me my coffin.*
Consummate salesman, he once spoke with verve about business, cavorted
with belief as passionate as a young Willy Loman—a real *old sport*
come of age playing hooky from McBurney School to inhale McSorley's,
jazz, cigs at the Village Vanguard, in training for three martini lunch glory.
The coffin portrait taken before he fled Manhattan, capitalist pilgrim
& flagship wife, selling our family business at forty-five, us children
securely away. His success bred a quiet discontent like the one percent's.
It rotted into compost for the secret life he grew. I tried to plant
new rows inside the long untended furrows. The distance to hell's fjord
in negative numbers. Whatever is rocky will have to produce its own reward.

Little did I guess my father's mistress was the pregnant red-head,

about my age, walking by my seat, like a newlywed to the newly dead.

One can only hope to be wise, to see what is right there, point of fact.

My aphasia always looks in the mirror of my lipstick compact.

We are all born of a history of long desires, a library of Harlequins

where good-boy sons work their way out of the old country of charlatans,

from Brooklyn to Scarsdale. In a nearby pew, stepmother rocked

regally as a prophet — none the wiser in her big hat, her cloisonné locket

filled with my dead father's hair. She knew witchcraft. She once buried

some of his mane with a red ribbon, three weeks later they were married.

Everafter, Delilah to Dad's Samson. I waited, stripped like a screw thread,

for him to regain his strength and leave her. Instead,

sixty-one years old, he keeled, cardiac arrest in the car, his main stage.

My cursive script a florid denial that I can live for him on a blank page.

Like him, I tend to imagine events as if they were counterfeit, not writ.

Once time was only a metaphor for money, now there are bitcoins.

In 1939, his Ashkenazi Father schlepped desks up Madison Avenue.

Always the bon vivant, pays for the party, never sends a check since he flew.

Mother complained of Dad, we were forced into affordable housing — oy vey.

When my stepmother appeared for one of our birthdays,

Mother marveled at her replacement. I eavesdropped her tale,

I wanted to be jealous, she said. My mother, beautifully male-female,

combination athletic lesbian, duty-honor-dinner party WASP. Mother

made things fun, but played it too butch to let me bake or sew or love her.

I yearned for pink dresses, frilly tennis pants, things that weren't cotton;

anything but the T-shirt I wore all fourth grade, sweaty, sodden. Its tenet:

A Woman's Place is in the House and in the Senate. I tried to schmooze

some gender roles from stepmother's straight girl stockpile, but she refused.

I did not marry your father for his money! Stepmother's operatic mantra

when tipsy—seems like the kind of ballad style song Sinatra

sang. I praise her excellent cooking, her Saint Francis love of animals,

her knowledge of Estee Lauder products, so fashionable it's laughable,

say nothing of her hoarding, her waning Farrah Fawcett style. Erstwhile,

Dad business-traveled out of the house, into a double life, stockpiled

other redheads, blondes. It is easier to play a role if it doesn't spill

into your real life. A good salesperson sees what's possible with a dollar bill.

Fridays, he'd return home to New Hampshire from the city with flowers —

commerce between his worlds, a toll he paid in sunflowers. A coward,

it wasn't clear to whom-what-where he belonged everywhere all at once.

A whole lot he wasn't telling me, stepmother guessed, a kind of dunce.

I recalled an elevator ride. I'd said: *I wish we were dead.* Silent as braille,

he walked out the door to the third floor, *never one for the hard sell.*

❧

One Sunday, I got a conference call from Mother, my siblings.
Your father had a pregnant mistress half his age. No kidding!
The pretty red-headed woman at the funeral. *He was going to play*
stay-at-home Dad for his final act. And not that they
ever helped us, but his notorious millions are missing —
your stepmother's flipped. Not to mention, she found medical
bills for a hush-hush heart attack he kept secret. Incredible!
The thing with drama is you always know
something is wrong but not what. Days later stepmother showily
announced her plan to exhume father from his burial plot
in New Hampshire, move him next to his parents in New York to rot.
The trouble was the lack of cash. What happened to millions
unresolved, even by detectives. I was sure the money cursed, its brilliance
held dominion for so long, now stepmother understood his lack of mercy —
how he looked through you like a window. I felt a dillydallying sympathy.

Each of us a cautionary parable. Money was the frayed rope

binding our family together, but in death Father read his horoscope,

became a trope. My inner Gollum savored his drifting. I liked

his freedom's permanent invisibility. It is only what we type

with our own ugliness that can turn to beauty. The bee

and its stinger. Though we won't meet, I hear his baby's

wails like a discordant jazz (rising over the village) that I will replay

gladly. Wherever she is she will never find him, he always drives away,

and she is a character in search of an author who can't tell this story

anymore. We don't exist in tandem with him, except in what I can say

on paper, written down. The Conjurer knows the curtain inters now

for later. The day is reckless, beginning again like a mistress. Somehow

everything is a stage marker: The lingering scent of his aftershave.

Stepmother refuses a headstone for Father's grave.

THREE

And a man newly dead would really know. And the poet would bear witness to that knowledge, if only he could work out the way of getting it.
— *Unknown*

REGARDING MY AUTOPSY

❧ I

When they pronounced me DOA, the glass doors

of the hospital opened for me like jaws,

as they rolled me to the morgue. I hovered

above the gurney sweet as marijuana smoke.

It was so black, the white sheet flimsy as a veil, slipping off me.

The spirit's permanent stutter, trying to get the unsaid out

into the reddening sky. The Velcro pull of soul from body —

the diving into darkness so chill it froze each query

at its birth — I thought where is my car? Where are my children?

The question was —

something I had to remember.

The glass doors swishing open and shut like a thresher.

But I kept forgetting —

how did I die?

ↈ II

On the clipboard. Other notes.

Item: One wallet, black, one hundred and twenty two dollars

Item: A gold wedding band, inscription 9/7/83

Item: one set of keys

Item: one roll of peppermint lifesavers, unopened

Item: Ray Ban aviator sunglasses, left side bent

Items: a beige V-neck sweater (ripped in front), tan khakis, blue button-down shirt (buttons missing), burgundy oxford shoes, brown leather belt

Above the Medical Examiner's table, a sign in Latin —

Hic locus est ubi mors gaudet succurrere vitae —

This is the place where Death rejoices to teach those who live.

His terrible angels *dream-hover taking notes:*

Desires 420 grams, ambitions 301 grams.

State of Grace: Limbo.

But the examiner's scalpel is sharper

than the divinest quill.

≈ III

Can you hear me?

    Yes. I can hear you.

Tell me what the report says.

    It says: Your heart weighs 290 grams. It says: congestive heart failure.

Are you sure? I see you in a summer field, Vermont a long time ago.

    Yes, I'm sure. Your heart was unsure.

I can smell the top of your infant head.

    Maybe you're death-dreaming.

I think you were my daughter. Didn't I teach you how to drive?

    That's what I'm saying.

IV

Then I owe you an apology.

I'm not sorry for my life ... but I'm sorry for something,

the other corpses in the morgue, still on their stretchers,

mock me with their decorous stillness, their hospital tubes and plastics,

the whites of their eyes have turned hen's egg brown.

The terrible angels wield their long tweezers,

strange extractors. I am weary —

the sensation I once had —

unable to stop, the toboggan threshing me down the hill —

please, if you are my daughter, conjure that which was once me

putting a soft blanket over you at midnight.

I've left you nothing but narrative to appease your afflictions —

CONDOLENCE IN CEMENT

Make your partings complete.
Don't roll them over and over

like a worry stone, until your hands are dry and cut,
your mind wave-worn as a cliff hit by incoming tides.

What's *goodbye* but a prayer for releasing
what has passed, as flowers send pollen into the wind?

Let your goodbyes be direct and clean as a master's
sketch, brush strokes that finally get the flower's

essence — art so true even we will believe
those marks on paper bloomed a flower.

Let it all be complete,
don't try to reverse what's been undone

with your thought's bulldozer. Make way –
even the future can't retrieve what's left behind,

the sealing cement poured in the gap:
More adamant than stone.

WILL

❧ 1.

Body became a blue Antarctic ice
I could never swim in, dive back into
that pooling of self and will.
I made appropriate provisions.

I ask only a stunted singing.
Pay my just debts, my funeral expenses,
my debt to star-gazing.

Any power of appointment at the time of my death shall be
as the moth's wings are, satiny, transparent,
their power rife from eating wool and cotton.

O, November, you're a cold one,
with your aluminum grayness,
your flat affections.

❧ 2.

A previous marriage ended in divorce produced
three children for which provisions were
made — skeletons filled
with tibia, scapula. Covered in silk, of dermis.

I have bequeathed to them each individually during my life-
time blood salt, blue-red.

✍ 3.

Even after death, I will still be
Battle-weary — the only thing

between me and nothing.
The Governing Law of this document —

the pressure of my spirit pushing
away from body. The exchange of light
and dust. That go-no-go tango.

Once I thought love was youth and spring,
but then the biblical and naphthalene smell

of heading off *moths and rust consume,*
and my third wife (my final bow) —
administer and dispose of said rest —
these orphaned glimpses of the past —

the children clutching my legs, walking
the dog down Jane Street, the gin smell

of the office, the lipstick kisses of secretaries, the terror
of a certain blue sky, the falling curtain of six p.m.

Each time I thought my life was beginning again —
the three seconds it took to consider *the terms and provisions thereof
as they may now complete* the picture

from the kitchen window — apple tree, stone wall, then everything
that can't be seen — the slow torture of what will
never happen fading into white across the blue
of sky where a hawk takes flight into —

the best of my knowledge of sane mind, under
no constraint or undue interference.

❧ 4.

O, November death,

walk me to the stony Connecticut
River where my tethered rowboat
splashed by one last surging,
secession of winter's dreadful
semi-colon.

It is raw here.

Soon I shall lift beyond
this unruly applause of north wind.

Cut the line for me, as I cannot,
so my boat can steady and hold
what's left of the will
before it slips to the other side —

I have set my hand and seal and swear —

In autumn's falling leaves no leaf
can unbrittle itself, once it has
been vain for that moment of glory before falling
and has subscribed —

our names as witnesses to the execution thereof.

FROM THE BOOK OF CONDOLENCES

The book forewarned: *You may have visions.*

You may think you hear your dead parents speaking in the courtyard.

On page fifteen it comforted: *Life is a process of second guessing oneself.*

It uncannily predicted: *You may be completely screwed.*

It offered irony and canned laughter*: Ha, ha, ha.*

It gave dubious advice: *Wait. There may be a way out, but*

the door has premonitions and is very fragile.

It asked: *Knock, knock. Who's there?*

On the cover, a picture: *The dead tiptoeing, startled like ballerinas.*

The book warned*: It is the pain of the absence of the body you will fear.*

It provided a clue*: Beware of a goblet filled to the brim with agony.*

It whistled*: The far water remembers. It pools and sings of the ransacker.*

The punch line was always: *Do not drink the story.*

WHAT DEATH SAID

1.

DEATH said:

Pull over to the side of the road.

Lewis Itkin felt pressure, splitting
    in his body's tectonic plates, a burning, a rawness
        like red ants carving up his arm.

DEATH said:

This heart attack involves only you.
Put the car in park; highway marker 324.

Lewis Itkin listened robotically, ruefully
    to DEATH's roust and pulled his white Mercury
        to the shoulder of I-95 North.

DEATH said:

Now close your eyes.
I'll tell you when to open them.

Then

2.

... a sort of sensory slide show, a pastiche of the past:

> Flies dive-bombing in late May,
> a broken canoe paddle,
> his old blue Schwinn —

> Two sunburned children tugging on his trouser leg —
> The sound of a cocktail party rising —

> Mercury balling, a broken thermometer,
> Mother with a cool compress —

❧ 3.

The wedging him open —

      All he could hear was a song in his head that had once annoyed him,

         the song helped him to resist,
         it threshed his mind…

DEATH said: It is true

    I am slave to fate, chance, kings, and desperate men.

         … AND in the background Lewis Itkin heard the state trooper smashing the windows of his locked, traveling salesman's car to carry his six foot three frame out onto the stretcher where the paddles zapped and zapped until a white feeling overcame him…

…He thought, there *is* a humming after all…

…How he had once found meditation impossible, but
         now its white noise was a lovely wall against
             pain's will; —

❧ 4.

DEATH said: *Here is where your heart stops, here at marker number 324, I-95 northbound lane, New Rochelle, New York, 10:32 a.m. EST, November 3, 2003.*

    … AND Lewis Itkin began to remember what he had forgotten those sixty years ago, when he chose this life, before the angel hit him and he forgot everything…

    … AND DEATH made Lewis Itkin take the first step in renouncing his self, and his soul began the slow rising of undoing and unchoosing — he thought briefly of that movie he liked, *The Red Balloon*.

    … AND the lighter he felt the more clearly he could see each of his children as if he were dreaming their lives …

5.

Lewis Itkin could still feel his mind,

    but where was his body?

For a few minutes he ghost-roamed the halls

    of his life. A sweet odor, like pomegranates or urine. The sun

hurt him as it shone through the four eyes of the house.

    In front of a mirror, only the heat of invisibility:

Lewis Itkin said, *So this is not you*, and the mirror said, *Yes, this is not you* …

    then he saw them for the last: They each stood

at the distance the living must take. A young woman

    (his eldest) in a green dress brushing her hair,

reciting from a poem: *Language wants to avert death.*

    The poem with a blue bicycle in it. How she couldn't stand the

rigorous impossibility of the everyday. He'd taught her that.

    Now he saw it amplified in his mind's eye: never enough

money, time, love, patience. She had married an older man,

and lived in an older house. Then,

by the light that came in through the half-shut door (his second child,

his second vision) rubbing her pregnant belly,

a little foot kicking. She had been the dutiful child, the good girl.

… AND then Lewis Itkin thought of his body alone, far from home,
at the morgue. Who would retrieve it? Who would dress it for burial?

A panic welled inside him and his blood began the pooling and stasis
of its death song no one but DEATH and GOD could finish.

๑ 6.

DEATH said: *Lewis, look here (into this embryo).*

> …AND like an ultrasound, DEATH made X-ray
> glasses so Lewis Itkin could see into the globe of his own
> beginning, his little skeleton, his wiry umbilical cord, his
> extra rib. A life he had been perpetually driving away from
> when the pressure in his heart popped open his ears so he
> could hear DEATH.

DEATH said: *Don't be alarmed. As we make our way out, gravity will
release you. Go with it. All is reversed.*

> …AND at that moment Lewis Itkin saw the X of
> his X, and the Y of his Y meet, then he felt a stillness, then
> the sound of film as it rolls and whips onto the spool.

DEATH said: *The end of you, Lewis Itkin.*

> …AND his soul finished lifting and ripped away.

His last thought was
> *how close I once was…*

> …AND his name was crossed out and shaken off of
> DEATH's palimpsest back into the field of names and
> matter where spiritual worker ants would begin to take his
> body speck by blessed speck to the place where the living
> can not go.

HOW TO SEW AN UNHEMMED DAY

Can you gather in sorrow's excess stratosphere? Evenly baste
the sky's regret? Do you know how to smock diminishment?
Embroider your way out? Have you a thimble? Check
in your little mending kit. Don't despair to protect yourself,
how about scissors to sever the binding thread? Clearly
you've lost your instruction
book and pattern.

Soon the night will unstitch from the sky's protective net,
this unrepairable blue, cloaking you in
blackness.

You won't remember the smell of your hair,
the curve of your waist.
Where are your spectacles?

Stitch quickly,
before the swatch of aquamarine fades.

AT THE SWATCH WATCH STORE
IN NEWARK'S TERMINAL C

I'm going home.
I look at Swatch watches
        at a store of timepieces for people who wait.

Once there was a purple inside space called deep of night
        where God's amygdala made time. The Newark moon
did not shine. No travel delays, all fine.

        The past kept living inside me
like a cheap Timex.
        "Where are you going?"

the store clerk said. But I heard my father in my head,
        practically dragging me from bed to bon voyage me
out of Newark when this terminal was merely stairs,

        no moving sidewalks, when we were people still,
not consumers, flying nineteen dollar flights into Burlington,
        Vermont on People's Express.

"Get your ass on the damn plane," my long dead father forever
        says in his Barry White voice, now just a floating bubble
above me like a cartoon, or a synapse, or a brain protein.

        "You're making me late," he says and waves, bye-bye.
Scotch still in my pores like milliseconds
        collecting for takeoff into minutes. O, briefcase:

The Wild Blue Yonder song he used to sing me.
        On my own. Then. Now. A store of timepieces
for those who wait. Once Amelia Earhart dedicated

this airfield and hangar. Deep inside God's amygdala,
I tick-tock. "I'm going. I'm going."
And he's gone into a parade of pinstripes.

I hold a Swatch watch. It has a big cherubic face
that says 11:11. The angels are watching.
They haven't aged. My hand to God's portal.

INVITATION TO MY REAL SELF
FROM MY IMAGINARY SELF

But I felt: you are an I,
you are an Elizabeth,
you are one of them.
      — Elizabeth Bishop

Please come flying: I've been to a wake and a funeral. The other
alters aren't as fun as you. As the host I invite you clearly, over the
Brooklyn Bridge, please come flying. So that when you arrive I will
know you've been listening to your iPod on the train, snapping Juicy
Fruit gum, committing the same old adultery in your head because
I am the host and you are the alter. Tonight we will be two characters
in search of an author, or maybe I mean father.

On this fine morning — the Peter O'Toole Suite in the Chelsea
Hotel is all ours, infamous, full of brightness, funky polka-dotted
bedspreads, an explosion of purple walls, where the great actor stays
when he's in town, the richness of his Brit lilt still echoing the halls —
I quoteth him here, father's favorite actor, stage and screen:

one who has adopted the theater as other people adopt the cloth…

Sometimes you try to deny my existence, but today please come
flying, so we may live truthfully under imaginary circumstances. You
are playing Salome on her divorce tour — and I am your sidekick, your
bff. I am wearing the ripped black ribbon of mourning because I am
the true identity responsible for our day-to-day functioning. While you
study Stanislavsky, wear red Chanel lipstick that I can't afford, and read
O'Toole quotes from old magazines:

Never choose the dumb waiter under Waiting for Godot for your
point of departure. This is a mistake. Brave mind you…

You want us to see Dutch domestic paintings, the giant Joan of Arc with her lacewings, nymphs in the big green room all at the MET. Fine: Art is where you want everything to be as evocative as possible. But I don't necessarily want it. I am a archetype, a stepdaughter, so I have the most problems with the accuracy of the setting: You think we are playing hipsters who just turned forty.

In the Peter O'Toole Suite — we converse with ghosts living and dead — old beatniks, psychics, skeptics, bootlicks, a few comics. O'Toole speaks in italics:

> *I once played the devoted school teacher in "Goodbye Mr. Chips"*
> *and a lovely schizophrenic in "The Ruling Class"…*

But the problem with drama is; Nothing ever ends. Whatever happens, will happen again after the matineé. O'Toole agrees with the pipes clanging us awake:

> *The dead want the living to learn from their bad timing —*
> *So isn't it time to start living as soon as you can? And then just*
> *keep your fingers crossed if you survive?*

Perhaps? Maybe?

Of course, a man newly dead would really know. And the poet would bear witness to that knowledge, if only he could work out the way of getting it.

> *Dangerously we would live, hysterically we agreed…*
> *we drank to our precarious healths and to that good ship Venus.*

I try to split from you as I have split from our others. I stare at the doorknob until I trance. Then I can be you again and check the doorknob lock thirteen times and wash hands five or ten times because anything can happen and sometimes does.

FOUR

The whole of America is a poem on how to read *Death of a Salesman.*
— unknown

WILLY: Biff Loman is lost. In the greatest country in the world a young man with such — personal attractiveness, gets lost. And such a hard worker. There's one thing about Biff — he's not lazy.

LINDA: Never.

WILLY: [*with pity and resolve*]: I'll see him in the morning; I'll have a nice talk with him. I'll get him a job selling. He could be big in no time.
— Arthur Miller, *Death of a Salesman*

WILLY LOMAN'S RECKLESS DAUGHTER

Prologue

Willy Loman's reckless daughter flies quietly,
fluttering like a silk-moth behind me

blocking my life, my scenes
in whichever stage direction she wants.

Sometimes at night I can feel her dialing into me,
her ringing calls like an imperial decree.

When she sleeps she crashes, like a car
into the guardrail of my ambition.

Her curse like a poison I cannot smell,
an asphyxiation of the self by the self, that hell and hard sell.

Split personalities, we dream through the night,
of our merger and acquisition, in her half-moon light,

Not even my husband can feel
her there between us — a secret contract under seal.

When I awaken, her irises touch mine;
an awful, indecipherable fault line.

She's a character in search of an author, a devotee,
trying to recount her history through me,

until I channel her. She's like a phantom limb,
hymn to the invisible. Her shameless whims,

the subtext of my lies. Under her tinted hair
the forest murmurs, becomes a thought, or prayer.

Until her thoughts tumble into mine;
colors bleed. In the morning, I'm overwrought —

My patrilineal kin, she begins to wear thin,
when she undoes hospital corners I've tucked so gently in.

Her cool white rising is meringue completing —
the high-pitched silence of our congealing.

She was always ceremonially unfolding
his white shirts, unpressing the folds

in my circumstance. I did and didn't want her. I kept
trying to catch her, then let her slip. Any intent

to have her near made her more invisible. Her electric
breasts overfilled my brassieres. An interaction, our dialectic —

She never removes her hat upon entering the door
to my personality. Ma semblable, ma soeur!

Act 1. At the Grave

O, Willy Loman, I'm your reckless daughter, your memento mori.
I'll never be a character in your authorized story,

the one that brought you fame.
No, no one knows my name,

a character in search of a moment
to come alive. I am your love accident.

I sneak into narratives,
As some do movies.

Here's a scene I saw
from the outside, like a reader in awe:

I hid behind a cemetery wall listening in
to the darkness, to the Requiem beginning

on page 137 of the Compass 1960 edition
of *Death of a Salesman*, where I hover like an apparition

of a character not seriously considered, a bastard erased,
in the name of good taste,

The funeral scene where Charlie
says to my half-brother Biff, unaware:

> *... for a salesman, there is no rock bottom to the life ...*
> *... a couple of spots on your hat, and you're finished.*

Watch me as the curtain rises on this poem, where I confess,
where you'll see me in my black mourning dress,

placing a small rock on your grave,
after your wife and sons have slouched away,

cawing *we're free, we're free,* like the crows
pecking the loose dirt, quid pro quo.

I pulled like gravity and pushed like wind,
Aching from the weight of all I thought I owned.

I tread this stage to keep walking directly into my fate —
a character meeting herself on a blind date,

that stage-left tempest: I am the lost daughter,
and now you are the lost father.

What did your God of the almighty dollar say to you
when you came to his pearly gates with your suicidal ballyhoo?

Did he give you a good review, a heavenly commission?
Put your sins in remission?

Alone in the taxi, I have a panic attack. Full of doubt:
will the widow find me out,

or the man who drives the hearse?
What will the busybodies think — or that audience, that curse?

Sometimes I'm ashamed, sometimes righteous. It's a dramatic art.
I raise my fist until anyone can see it's a heart.

I have a feeling that's what drama is:
the line no one wants to write or live.

Act 2. The Secret Child

How I tire of being the secret child,
reviled, slightly wild.

The geography of hotel rooms, diners, gas stations
map out my psyche, my motivations.

The secret child written out of the narrative thread,
so I must rise to my persona from a kind of living dead,

because whoever has the luck to be born
a living character can laugh at death. No need to heed the lovelorn

curtain calls, Daddy, in the backstage of your *other* life
for right now, *the woman has come from behind the scrim*

and is standing, putting on her hat, looking
into a mirror and laughing.

It's my mother (your Boston lover), just before
I grow inside her — a fetal saboteur.

Hers is the back-story of your drama, where
she's knocked up, unsure. Then out of thin air —

how the one time your son Biff came to visit you
at your hotel, and found the two of you trying to screw.

> *Biff: Somebody in there?*
> *Willy: No, that was next door.*

Willy bursts out laughing. Biff joins him.

Your son witnessing my mother in cherry red,
laughing, tumbling from her hiding spot, back onto your bed.

He sees only the blonde wisps of mother's hair,
her sexy pout. No matter who plays Biff,

he's always angry over having found you out.
He doesn't know the weight pressing down on him is me.

Act 3. As Pure as Ocean Glass

The laughing and crashing, the oceanic abyss
of your adultery, yawps inescapably before me.

Driving to your funeral doing one hundred
and ten — another desire thundering —

strumming me with staying power:
disaster waiting for the zero hour

when the fatherless daughter makes bad choices,
sleeping with any one with deep voices.

Someone who says *I love you: No, really. I do!*
Reckless, feckless, hell on burning wheels going through.

I look like you, the real deal.
A shrimp! An angel!

I'm filled to the brim with you: Your perversions,
diversions, fusions, revisions.

A child of narrative like everyone else,
only I've got a stutter that troubles.

Maybe it was the midwife washing me
at birth, vinegar, water, maybe.

On the way back from the home
for knocked up gals like Mother, how

she performed a spell to heal my belly button over, made a space
so blank, I bore no trace from the human race.

Act 4. Tried On So Many Faces, Used Them All

When this scene opens on you in your two piece suit,
a melody is heard, played upon a flute,

and the curtain rises, as I give my next soliloquy
from my parallel world, my abyss.

I, too, sell on the road, that endless roundabout.
I deal you, Father. Already, I sold-out

once for twenty bucks, to a fool —
a football player at school.

I sold Girl Scout cookies, steaks, vacuums, drapes,
open windows to prisoners, your stash of sour grapes.

I sold my song at midnight, straight from its jar,
to the three drunks left at the bar.

I'm a wandering heart that can't rest.
Two parts real, one part unreal. My test:

I climbed the bean tree.
I drank the Kool-Aid.

I marketed it: Money, love, appointments, clients —
on the road, the car counts miles like a child through each ZIP code.

Back and forth, Boston, New York,
doppelganger in a family of doppelgangers. Such torque:

The road is my memory.
Come on, Willy, sell me

a story. What does it take
to become an A-1 fake?

A laugh in the throat instead of the belly,
or blind, unkind ambition, the quick Machiavellian

charm that worms? You told me to: write thoughtful cards,
send gifts, always smile, chat, never disregard

other's interests, read *How to Win Friends, Influence
People* or *The Religion of Sales*. I've tried on so many faces,

used them all.
The (*Curtain*) is my veil.

Act 5. To Further Understand I May Not be Human at All

Every salesman tries on so many faces,
they lose their own in the road's empty spaces.

I was a secret stuck inside a secret. You kept
tabulating yourself in me. I wept

for the curtain's endless rising
on your death. The morning shining

in through the kitchen window.
The past could not enter, nor foreshadow.

I stood at the sink,
wanting a tall, strong drink,

my hands in water, dish soap sparkling,
the pop of the moment undoing

itself. Diderot said, We girls all die at fifteen,
yes, I believe in that, and living unseen.

Grandfather always scolded: You're nothing but a party girl,
all swirl and frill but what have you got to show? That's no way

to break the paternal mold. The window looked in on me without
sympathy; the streetlight whimpered to the street.

Like you, father, I took the open road into my arms,
meant to avoid harm — my incantation:

Let's go. I let the umbrage of halogens rain down,
swimming through them to tomorrow and tomorrow,

another sale where I become
my product, or it becomes me.

Thundering demands hammer us down,
so no human can rebound,

except to stare in the mirror at what's lost:
no longer being human is the cost.

Act 6. Another Day, Another Dollar

Your passing a dollar bill over the counter
makes us intimate.

I am the exchange, the wheel,
the scent of money: How I feel

when I sell women's suits
along the routes you took.

Come touch this cotton made
from the finest grade of Egyptian flower.

The magic of my marketing, I can make anyone
feel the need shimmying up the stalk inside.

Watch Willy as I unhinge the dread
that's locked inside my buyers' heads.

I am the equation calculating
your marketing profile and going rate,

I can sum up your soul — no fingers
no calculator — wholly in my head.

New York City of hard knocks,
Boston, Providence, New Haven,

Waterbury, city of clocks.
I watch miles pile up like wrecks.

As I pass the test of full commission —
note cards in my purse with client likes

and dislikes; I keep conversation chits
like some women keep Advil or lipstick,

Prozac, condoms, or holy water —
I'm Willy Loman's reckless daughter,

once you promised me a hammock
to swing between our walnut trees,

but you left after a quick ice cream
with your fraudulent schemes and bogus

American dream. Your tales of the road I travel now.
In the famous story of your life (don't take a bow),

it was your sons, Biff and Hap, you once
promised a hammock. Tell me, Willy, isn't it true —

daughter sounds like slaughter,
son, the sun. Now I see,

you grew tired from the double life —
the driving and the dropping off, the cliff

of double-family strangeness — your
schmoozing couldn't heal the rift

that widened between us, the ditch;
where you and your car get stuck.

You wanted to speak to anyone but me, reach
across the empty space and grab someone else's hand

and shake it hard. Someone who didn't know your game,
or lack of shame, what you'd do for an insurance claim.

You told me to find a nice man, settle down,
but I hound you on the Mass Pike, town after town,

but we're both ghosts and both undone,
our reflections vanish in unforgiving sun.

Sitting roadside staring at the blue Taconic Range
I feel deranged, I smell of cigarettes and death.

I've won a regional sales prize,
still I'm devoted to your lies,

your shadow, the quiet, the quest
for cash, the flow of a different story.

I can't settle into any life, I'm a coward
like you. My reckless coming and going leaves a wake

from the man in Waterbury's chiming clocks,
to one in Providence drinking champagne,

where in the hotel room, in vain,
we heard the ambulance take the pain

of the salesman's heart attack leaving the room
with a drowsy truth the cleaning lady found looming.

We heard he lived, saw his business card each week on the concierge
desk for the dinner-for-two drawing, until the demiurge

of that singular hour, shook and shuffled
his cards. Like you, exited, stage left, one day, *the car speeds off,*

the music crashes down in a frenzy of sound,
which becomes the soft pulsation of a single cello string.

The (scrim, no...) *Curtain* (or is it...veil?
mirror not reflecting?) *Falls.*

NOTES

"Living Truthfully Under Imaginary Circumstances" is an expression coined by Sanford Meisner to describe his approach to and goal for American acting. The poem owes its existence to the acting techniques that it seeks to re-enact, especially the works of Sanford Meisner. In addition, the poem's philosophy is rooted, in part, in *Process and Reality* by Alfred North Whitehead.

"Where moths and rust consume" comes from King James Version of the New Testament Bible, Matthew 6:19-20.

The quotation, "slave to fate, chance, kings, and desperate men" is from "Death Be Not Proud: Holy Sonnet X" by John Donne.

In "Willy Loman's Reckless Daughter" the phrase "ma semblable, ma soeur is from Adrienne Rich's poem, "Snapshots of a Daughter-in-Law," a feminist variation on Charles Baudelaire's phrase, "mon semblable, mon frère" in "Au Lecteur (To the Reader).

"Under her tinted hair the forest murmurs" is from Simone de Beauvoir's "The Second Sex."

This entire book is in love with *Death of a Salesman* by Arthur Miller, and has been in conversation with it for a good, long time.

ABOUT THE AUTHOR

Elizabeth A. I. Powell is the author of *The Republic of Self*, which received the New Issues Poetry Prize, selected by C. K. Williams. Her work has appeared in the *Pushcart Prize Anthology 2013*, as well as *Academy of American Poets, Alaska Quarterly Review, Barrow Street, Black Warrior Review, Ecotone, Harvard Review, Handsome, Hobart, Indiana Review, The Missouri Review, Mississippi Review, Ploughshares, Post Road*, and elsewhere. She is Editor of *Green Mountains Review*, and Associate Professor of Writing and Literature at Johnson State College. She also serves on the faculty of the low-residency MFA in Creative Writing at the University of Nebraska-Omaha and the Vermont College of Fine Arts MFA in Writing and Publishing. Born in New York City, she has lived in Vermont since 1989.